Please return or renew this item before the latest date shown below

Renewals can be made
by internet   www.fifedirect.org.uk/libraries
in person   at any library in Fife
by phone   08451 55 00 66

Thank you for using your library

© Christopher Harvie
2013

First edition 2010
Argyll Publishing
Glendaruel
Argyll PA22 3AE
Scotland
www.argyllpublishing.co.uk

The author has asserted
his moral rights.

**British Library
Cataloguing-in-
Publication Data.
A catalogue record for
this book is available
from the British
Library.**

ISBN 978 1 908931 19 1

Printing:
Martins-the-Printers,
Berwick

in memory of
Angus Calder,
historian, and
John Burnie,
engineer

Contents

Preface

IN 2010, I tried to write an account of Scotland which conveyed the basic historical facts. It stemmed from my realisation, talking to schools as a Member of the Scottish Parliament from 2007-2011 and showing visitors around, that not enough had been done to make either group aware of the narrative of the country's history. So it's meant to be read by those of all ages coming to it for the first time.

Scottish history suffers from Anglocentrism – you could call it 'metromania' – to the degree that you can't extract a believable Scotland from most 'British' histories. And you therefore can't relate the country to great historical, economic and cultural movements which swept over the world – many of which it influenced. I have tried to give a robust account, with an easily accessible 'bookstore', and a guide to accessible sources, illustrative material and historical sites. A summing-up traces the interweaving of what Edwin Muir called 'the story and the fable' and shows how, in teaching history, we can match the local to the global.

The book shares the sources and therefore debts to colleagues and friends who helped in my *Short History of Scotland,* Oxford, 2002 (you know who you are) but is a reinterpretation with young people and visitors in mind. So it was rethought and written in trains and buses and bed-and-breakfasts, and owes much to the ingenuity of publisher Derek Rodger: not least the contribution of Scoular Anderson. Thanks also to Logie Barrow, Stefan Buettner and Alice Lowenstein for their help in updating and revising this second edition.

Are books dead? Have the web and handheld taken over? No they've not. They're awkward to use *and* take notes from; they break down. You can't use them in the bath. Clan Scotland books, of which this is the first, are a shot at combining history, directory and notepad. Here you'll find the basic facts, maps, websites: 'guid gear in sma' buik' written by someone who has taught and written on Scotland for forty years, with you in mind as student, businessperson, tourist.

Revisiting my 2010 text didn't just involve tackling mistakes and writing more directly. I also had to catch up not just with a changing present but, though genetic and archaeological progress and environmental history, with a better-understood remote past.

Christopher Harvie
Melrose, 2nd November 2012

PART 1
THE COMMUNITY
OF THE REALM

So was it, when of old each land,
A prey to every spoiler's hand,
Its ancient laws and rulers lost,
The Scot alone could freedom boast!
The Goth, the Saxon, and the Dane
Poured on the Scot their powers in vain;
And the proud Norman met a foe
Who gave him equal blow for blow.

George Buchanan, 1558,
translated by
Peter Hume Brown

The Romans invaded Scotland in 43AD
– did it rain all the time?

1. Fireball to Britannia

BC 10,000 to AD 500

IN THE eighteenth century there was a great debate over the origins of our earth. Did it evolve from a fireball or a mudball? The first group, the Vulcanists, was headed by the Scot, James Hutton, the second, the Neptunians, by the German Abram Werner. The prize went to the Vulcanists and their fiery mass which, over thousands of millions of years, cooled, solidified, acquired moisture and ultimately sustained life. In this process, Hutton's homeland was where tectonic plates of consolidated magma drove into one another, forcing themselves into a contorted, complex geology, one of the oldest parts of the earth. Much of the country's subsequent history depended on this, and the minerals and workable stone which was forced to the surface.

A series of ice ages incised the ravaged coast of the west, eroded sands from volcanic rock, whose deposits were progressively compressed and eroded again. Glaciers gouged valleys, their immense weight crushed the rotted remains of plants and trees, shells and early animals into limestone and coal.

Around 70,000 BC, proto-human 'Neanderthaler' primates made their way from Africa to the 'British' land-mass. Then, around 24,000 BC, the earth's orbit changed. The North Pole moved southwards and the region, at under-60 degrees Celsius, become crowned by a mile-deep ice-cap, driving early man back. When this melted, a few thousand Cro-magnon folk, also from Africa (and some part-Neanderthaler) turned up about 12,500 BC, crossing from Europe but stopping at the huge glacier that cut from the Severn to the Humber.

They reached Scotland about 10,500 BC in search of animals for food, furs and hide for boatbuilding and settlements. By 9000 BC they planted and milled, built in wood and stone, clearing much of the forest and tundra that replaced the ice – the later Great Caledonian Forest was something of a myth. Horses first appeared around 3000 BC, in the Paleolithic age, with its great stone monuments. Were these a means of keeping time? Or did a priestly element create ritual sites and temples to great leaders? Or did they simply mark separate identity? – like the Callanish stone circle in Harris, the tomb of Maeshowe or Ness of Brogar in Orkney, now thought to have influenced Stonehenge.

> 1200-1850 was 'The last Little Ice Age', with the seas being 5 degrees celsius cooler between 1560 and 1750 than they are today.

They were as intelligent as us – see mummified 'Otzi' of 3300 BC – though checked by short lives, lack of mobility and sophisticated technology, and since only a third of Scotland was under 150 metres (unlike most of England and Ireland), they were also hindered by cold and a lowland which was generally swamp or impassable scrub. The Skara Brae settlement on treeless Orkney (2000 BC), used stone panels as we would use an Ikea flat-pack, and long-vanished wood-working was probably equally ingenious. Callanish or Maeshowe may have gone from keeping time to cult centres; with regional monarchies giving way, in the bronze and iron ages (after 1500 BC), to independent farms and villages, with their dispersed weaponry, defensive fortresses and enclosures. Again, our images are filtered through the 'conjectural history'.

National myths may also reflect something more complex. Adam Smith's *The Wealth of Nations*, 1776, saw the origins of international trade in the eastern Mediterranean, coexisting with the Scots self-image of a folk who migrated from Scythia in Asia Minor. The reality was the westward conquest of the Celts of Hallstatt and La Tene (named after great hoards in Austria and Switzerland) about 800-500 BC. The Greeks who pushed them (500-100 BC) were – with

Scotland may be small, but its people's interest
in geography, trade and travel has marked the
globe, both directly and through the maps and

the geographer Ptolemy of Alexandria's map of 150
BC – the first to record the result of a circum-
navigation of the archipelago that the Romans would
know as Britannia.

The Roman invasions from 43 AD pushed deep into
Scotland and then stabilised themselves on the
fortified wall of Hadrian between Tyne and Solway,
built in 121 AD. Northward of this were the *Foederati*,
the 'Treaty people', a mix of Celtic tribes: Welsh
(Pretani) in the south-west, Scottish (Irish) in the
west, and north of the Forth the Picti, the least accessible by sea and consequently the most mysterious.

As early as this, some enduring elements of place
and people were being made clear. Scotland was easy
to invade, as long as sea-power was secured. The
west coast was a better bet than the east; it had plenty
of landmarks and sheltered waters. But there the
easy part ended, particularly for a great land power
like Rome. Aside from sea and land problems, the
natives were problematic. Some of the *Foederati* were
local allies: farmers, friendly and biddable, up for
villas and wine and a quiet life near Roman roads,
forts and ports; but others were herdsmen and
fishermen, rustlers and pirates (given a chance) and
a pest. The goodwill of the first wasn't worth the

atlases turned out by Scots firms such as Bartholomew, Johnston, Nelson. The Ordnance Survey started here, after 1745.

---

trouble-making of the second. For nearly 300 years (the length of the 1707-1997 Union) 'the last of the free' were contained, occasionally invaded and occupied as far as the Forth-Clyde Antonine Wall (142-185 AD) but largely left alone.

The Roman Empire was essentially land-based, founded on roads, camps and a well-organised army. In 314-24 AD it was nominally Christianised by the Emperor Constantine, who also shifted its centre to Constantinople (now Istanbul). But this eastern move made it also increasingly subject to the movements of peoples.

Enter, again, the weather factor. A 'little ice age' ended around 300 AD and in the Baltic area the Saxon peoples began to move westwards. In Britannia they found suspicion but also a welcome and were in places incorporated into the Roman system and army. The latter, however, grew more and more troublesome as central control deteriorated. Revolts brought minor officers to power, the gentry in their villas tired of the upstarts, and the departure of the legions from Britannia in 410 AD was therefore not seen at the time as a disaster. Until, of course, the whole centralised system fell apart.

'From the fury of the Northmen, Lord God deliver us!'

2. A Kingdom of Five Peoples

500 to 1066

WHAT FOLLOWED in the small Scottish lordships, paradoxically, wasn't the so-called Dark Ages but an astonishing creative output, which reached its climax in seventh century Iona in the illuminated books of Kells and Durrow, and the 'speaking' crosses of Celtic-Pictish Christianity. In the fifth century the Romano-British order was pressed by the Saxons to the islands and mountains of the west in the period of St Ninian, St Patrick and St Mungo (mythic figures based on the activity of real priests, travelling between now-isolated Christian communities). Then, using the sea and rivers, the Celtic church undertook energetic missionary activity which covered – and converted – much of western Europe.

This was a distinctive social order: herdsmen, fishers and subsistence farmers whose priestly leaders ranged from scholars or hermits to diplomats involved with the clans and small kingdoms. The

Population: perhaps 200,000 under the
Romans, rising to 0.6 million before the Black
Death, 1350, then falling to 0.5m in 1500. In
1755 (unofficial census) 1.25m, 1801 (first

Irish warrior-chief Columba of the Ui Neil (521-97) turned holy man and established his monastic enclosure on the island of Iona in Dal Riata, later bringing the Pictish kingdom to the east, centred on Inverness, into the Christian sway.

Columba's biographer Adamnan publicised pilgrim travel to the Holy Land and established a principle of consideration for civilians in time of war: a first step in international law. This success, based on the sea-lanes and the wood-framed, skin-clad galley (rather like the Irish 'curragh') ended with the creation under the family of Kenneth McAlpin of a unified kingdom of the Picts and Scots, around 850, responding first to Northumbrian and later to Viking invasions, which began at the end of the eighth century.

The Northmen – Vikings was a later term – in their 'hydrodynamic' longships, swift under sail or oar, wooden clinker planking secured by iron nails, worked as great a revolution in Europe as Moslem cavalry did at the same time with their thoroughbred horses. Their initial raids were brutal thievery – 'From the fury of the Northmen, Lord God deliver us!' – but were soon followed by trade and religious conversion, and a powerful elite rule ranging from northern

official census) 1.6m, in 1901 4.6m and in 2001 5.1m. Emigration has cut most of the natural increase: Sweden, 4.5m in 1901, went to 9m in 2010.

France to Sicily and Russia. They settled in Orkney and Shetland and along the western seaboard, which became a junction for further colonies in the Faroes, Iceland, Greenland and briefly 'Vinland' in North America. Their sagas, notably the *Heimskringla* (c.1230) showed a complex proto-democratic politics (the first parliament was at Thingvellir in Iceland in 930) and their influence on Scotland was great, although Orkney and Shetland didn't become Scots until 1472.

The outcome of this period was remarkable: the creation of a political structure that stretched across five ethnic groups – Scots, Picts, Britons, Inglis and Norse, and held them in some sort of unity. This was unique in early medieval Europe, and its imperial pretension was apparent in the names – David (Israel), Constantine (Rome), Alexander (Greece), Robert (Sicily) – the Scots kings gave themselves. The way they were elected was less inspirational – the general practice was a short, sharp war which established the best-qualified.

The last of these Celtic kings was Macbeth (1040-57), a reasonable ruler – first Scots king to visit Rome – but vilified by Shakespeare. He was overthrown by Malcolm III, married to a princess of the Saxon royal line. Malcolm would fall, raiding into England, in 1093.

Out of the feuding of Norman (and Scots) families
comes a nation

3. Living with Norman England

1066 to 1320

WITH KING MALCOLM and Margaret – she was later made a saint and her tomb at Dunfermline became a great place of pilgrimage – and their son David I, Scotland moved towards a more centralised, religiously-sanctified monarchy, with a southern border running along the ridge of the Cheviot Hills. But it was still a system distanced from that prevailing in England, in which the Norman Duke William rapidly pushed out the Saxon nobility after the Battle of Hastings in 1066.

Anglo-Norman nobles and merchants from France, Brittany and Flanders (some held land in England as vassals, or subjects, to its king) were partly countered by the Scots kings' careful cultivation of the church through building monasteries. Meanwhile the power of the Pope was growing, expressed in the ultimately brutal First Crusade (1096-99) and throughout the twelfth century. In 1175, a weak moment for the Plantagenet monarchs of England, the Scots persuaded Rome to recognise the Archbishopric of Glasgow as a 'special daughter': directly under Rome instead of under the English Archbishop of York. They would make much use of this in future, as well as of a 'parliament' where clergy sat with nobles.

At this date more than half of the population spoke Gaelic, with Inglis confined to the south-eastern part and the more northerly coasts with which it communicated. Berwick, on the English border was the largest town, one of those given the status of burghs by King David, chiefly as a means of raising royal revenue from an establishment of immigrant merchants. After 1314 the burghers entered Parliament as the 'third estate'.

The twelfth and thirteenth centuries were a period of peaceful coexistence between the two countries, although the Scots found themselves being embroiled in the unstable politics of the south. The latter part of the thirteenth century, however, saw a new purposiveness in English policy, with the career of Edward I.

Edward had crusaded, and stabilised his Norman inheritance in Gascony (South-Western France). In the 1280s he conquered the Welsh. He personified

> 'If a man were permitted to make all the ballads, he need not care who should make the laws of a nation.'
>
> Andrew Fletcher of Saltoun, 1704

modernising, integrating nationalism and he did not intend to stop at Wales when he was given his chance by the accidental death of Scots king, Alexander III in 1385. Alexander's heiress was the daughter of the Norwegian king, but she died on the sea crossing. Edward was then asked to arbitrate between the various claimants to the Scots throne, and in 1292 chose the most pliable, John Balliol. But after humiliations from Edward, Balliol treated for alliances with France and Norway. The French alliance, later denoted the 'Auld Alliance' of 1295, would last until the Reformation of 1560.

The kingdom of France expanded westward after 1200 from land around and east of Paris, but was still threatened by family rifts and the English in Gascony. It was not able to do much to help the Scots. Edward invaded, sacked Berwick and occupied the lowlands. The nobles were divided, many fancying their own families' chances under him. His problem was that war was all right when it paid for itself, but once an army had to be kept in the north, the exchequer was under pressure both from parliament and from ship-owners and contractors. Probably for this reason, Edward was particularly ruthless, seeking a rapid knockout before he ran into more trouble with France.

The Scots mobilised a 'national army' under Sir Andrew de Moray and William Wallace, and in 1297 inflicted a severe defeat on Edward's army at Stirling Bridge, the key junction-point between the Lowlands and Highlands. Moray represented the north, Wallace Lanarkshire: they indicated that the struggle was not a family one, but something like a national resistance. Wallace was later given the style of 'Guardian of Scotland', a national hero, while de Moray, who died of wounds, was forgotten.

Two further invasions took place, Edward throwing in troops from Gascony and Wales. His longbowmen defeated Wallace's 'schiltrons' (packed masses of spearmen) at Falkirk. Wallace was hunted down, betrayed in 1305, and brutally executed in London.

Robert Bruce, Earl of Carrick, then proclaimed himself king. Edward retaliated against Bruce's kinsmen. What had started as a family feud became, through Bruce's tactical skills and Highland alliances, a conflict raging throughout the country.

Edward organised a final invasion in 1307, but died at Burgh-by-Sands, near Carlisle. His son Edward II, first Prince of Wales, called it off, but returned in 1314 to relieve his garrison at Stirling

Castle. Bruce had by then either defeated or converted his rivals in the north and Hebrides, and just south of Stirling at Bannockburn, defeated a larger Edwardian force by making skilful use of terrain and traitors in the enemy ranks.

The War of Independence would go on and only be 'won' after Bruce's death in 1328, but it produced in 1320 a literary monument which would set the tone of the country's politics far beyond its time and place. The letter of the Scots nobles, clergy and 'community of the realm' to Pope John XXII, called the Declaration of Arbroath, endorsed King Robert, but ended with the ringing words:

For we fight not for honour or glory but for freedom, which no good man gives up but with his life.

Its ideas came from the supporters of Thomas a Becket against King Henry II, and the stirring passage may be from Dante's *Purgatorio*, but it seemed to symbolise a new and more democratic idea of nation and liberty. The new Pope ignored it, but it was translated into Scots and incorporated into Archdeacon Barbour's epic *The Brus* in 1375. Such poetry would become central to the Scots' heritage.

'Salmon, hides, wool out, silks and books in.'
Terms of trade are fun for the Scots nobility.

24

4. Auld Alliance and New Learning

1328 to 1541

IN 1359-60 vast impersonal forces struck again when the bubonic plague swept across Europe, cutting populations down by between a third and a half. Scotland seems to have got off fairly lightly, because its people were thinly distributed. There were then about 600,000: perhaps a quarter died. This may have meant that an older social order persisted longer than elsewhere in Europe, where the 'Black Death' led to economic change and the early development of 'proto-industrialisation' – a capitalism based on agricultural settlements and domestic industrial production.

In Scotland, the alliance with France – which plague hit as badly as England – would continue until 1560. This did little for trade, which stagnated, while the Scots pound fell. The only time that French troops were stationed in Scotland, in the late fourteenth and mid-sixteenth centuries, they were resented almost as much as the English, in the latter case even more.

But the alliance gave chances to the ambitious and educated: as mercenaries and scholars and lawyers in the service of the French king. It was from the Universities of Paris and the 'French' Popes at Avignon that careers were possible which were unthinkable in Scotland, and in due course these bred innovations at Scottish Universities such as St Andrews (1411), Glasgow (1451) and Aberdeen (1495).

In 1485 the Scots Church was finally given metropolitan status, although in fact this opened it to the greedy fingers of the royal family and the greater nobles. 'Bonds of manrent' – somewhere between insurance covenant and oath – provided security to the middling folk in a society where 'kin', 'clan' and 'family' counted a great deal.

The style of the French came north in the fashions and food of the court – particularly a taste for Bordeaux wine, the sophisticated design of Scots buildings such as the royal palaces of Linlithgow, Falkland and Holyrood, and an awareness of the European Rennaisance. In the fifteenth and early sixteenth centuries, when England was disadvantaged by civil war and regional risings, Scottish literature and poetry in particular – personified by King James I, William Dunbar, Robert Henryson, Bishop Gavin Douglas – was among the most advanced in Europe in terms of content, language and rhyme-scheme.

This did little for the ordinary Scots folk, over 80% of them still living on the land in townships of 12-15 families, cultivating their strip-fields with cumbersome ox-ploughs. But it seems the Scots thrived on diets which included a lot of meat and fish: not something that would last.

Trade had been restricted by the hostile country that now lay between Scotland and Europe, but urban life had started to develop an economic culture of its own, based on exporting wool, salted salmon and animal skins (for leather-tanning), and importing metal and luxury goods. The royal family settled on Edinburgh as a highly favoured capital, providing the city with increased opportunities and prosperity. In the Low Countries the Scottish staple (a trading centre of Scots citizens observing Scots Law) moved in 1540 from Bruges to Dutch Veere, in Zealand, where it would stay until 1799.

The Stewarts – the name suggests their origin as court officials (stewards) – succeeded the ailing grandson of the Bruce in 1406. The five successive Jameses proved an intelligent dynasty, and through hard-fought military campaigns gradually freed themselves from over-mighty nobles like the Douglases or the MacDonald Lords of the Isles who ruled large tracts of the country as if they were personal property.

Overall, Stewart pretensions frequently proved risky. This grandeur can still be seen in the complex spires of St Giles, Edinburgh and Linlithgow Kirks, and the University of Aberdeen: imperial crowns which underlined the dynasty's intention of cutting a dash in Europe. This was easier than taking on the English directly: the north of England was far poorer than the Scottish borders, and most Scottish invasions ended in defeat, often catastrophic, and bruising counterattacks. Once the English withdrew from France in 1453 (and the Turks took Constantinople), sorting out 'big nation' politics took centre stage. In the British Isles, Scotland would be under increasing threat.

This coincided with the zenith of the Stewarts under James IV (1488-1513), intelligent and progressive, cultivated and arrogant: the would-be founder of a Scottish navy. He was initially diplomatic enough to get power over the Church into his own

Stewart or Stuart? The first was original, Stewart meaning 'steward' in Scots. The French hadn't a 'w' so Mary of Guise and her daughter rejigged the name to Stuart.

hands, and to conclude a treaty of perpetual peace with King Henry VII of England, new, Welsh and uneasy. In 1502 James married Henry's daughter Margaret in the 'Union of Hearts'. The court historian John Maier wrote a wish-fulfilling *History of Great Britain*. But a revival of Anglo-French hostilities after the accession of Henry VIII led to a rash royal raid into Northumberland in 1513 which ended in disaster on Flodden Field.

Technology again favoured the English: artillery and musketry cut down James and his Scots nobility. As with Edward I, defeat led again to a systematic attempt to entrench English advantage which rebounded on itself. The Scots people resisted and forced the English back – the enduring local patriotism of the Border 'Common Ridings' at Hawick and Selkirk dates from this time – but James V's attempt to invade a now Protestant England ended in defeat at Solway Moss in December 1542. He died only a few days later, leaving his widow Mary of Guise and a baby daughter, Mary, in France.

'Wrong but romantic.' Schiller, Verdi and Hollywood get
Mary Stuart into the movies

5. Rough Wooing and Reformation

1542 to 1603

THE TUDORS had modernised their state and were now a formidable force, making their way in a Europe divided by Martin Luther's Reformation, 1517-28. In 1534-6 Henry VIII split from the church of Rome because his queen, the Emperor Charles V's sister, could not give him a male heir. The Pope, Charles' subject, would not allow an annulment of his marriage, but divorce was forced and in 1532 Henry married Anne Boleyn, who gave birth in 1533 to Elizabeth. No male heir, so she was executed.

In 1543, with a son (Edward, born 1537, died 1552) by his third wife, Jane Seymour, Henry tried to renew the union project. Not famous for tact, he chose a scorched earth policy and effectively drove the Scots into the arms of the French. Under the Regency of the Earl of Arran, the infant Queen of Scots was sent to France and betrothed to Dauphin

John Wycliffe's translation of the Bible in English
circulated in Scotland after 1409, and William
Tyndale's printed versions after 1525. James VI's

Francis in 1548. The widow of James V, Mary of
Guise, became Queen Regent in 1554.

But France's influence meant ironically that Scots
supped with the prophets of the reformed faith at
French universities. The Scots Reformation, when it
came, would take after the sophisticated urban
Calvinism of Paris, Amsterdam and Geneva, not a
monarch-driven attempt to repair a corrupt domestic
Catholicism after half a century of royal and noble
pillage.

In fact there was little enough about ideas on either
side: Mary of Guise and her daughter were clever,
tactically flexible, and (compared with the Tudors)
killed only a few protestants. Likewise, the grand
Scottish nobles manoeuvred shrewdly. In 1560 the
Earl of Hamilton (despite being Duke of Chatel-
herault) went over to the Lords of the Congregation,
who had backed reformist preachers like John Knox
and Andrew Melville. They thought France and Rome
worse than the English, so they leagued with them at
Berwick in February 1560, and ended the Auld
Alliance by the Treaty of Edinburgh in July.

This was the country to which Mary Queen of Scots
returned in 1561, as widow of her young French king.
Athletic, healthy and amorous, she outmanoeuvred

> decision to announce a new translation was made at Burntisland in 1601 and completed in England in 1611.

some reformers and married her cousin Henry Darnley in 1565. Mary bore a son but got caught up in court intrigue as Darnley became unstable, and was murdered in February1567 – the consequence of an alleged plot involving the protestant Earl of Bothwell, who became first her lover, then her husband. Forced to abdicate in July that year, Mary's lengthy career as a scheming prisoner in England eventually led Elizabeth, Queen of England, to have her executed in 1587.

A Reformation Parliament in August 1560 had separated Scotland from Rome with the 'Confession of Faith', but the *First Book of Discipline*, a blueprint for a 'Godly Commonwealth' based on a pyramid of parishes, presbyteries, synods (equal to bishoprics), with a General Assembly of the Kirk at the summit, remained declaratory. The Reformation was driven by the towns and the 'bonnet-lairds', taking a long time to spread to the third of the folk who still spoke Gaelic. Reformers ran into conflict with the nobility, but the educational ambitions survived, producing an Act anent Education in 1595 which promised a school in every one of Scotland's 1800 parishes.

Jamie the Saxt approached all problems
with an open mouth, but lived

34

6. The Wisest Fool

1603 to 1625

MARY'S INFANT SON, James VI, was thrown about like a ball between feuding nobles, and interfering English and French. His tutor George Buchanan, Europe's greatest classicist and a theoretical republican, beat him. In 1580, at the age of fourteen, James began to assert himself, increasingly conscious that he was the legitimate heir of Elizabeth (age 47 and still childless). English (if not Scots) monarchic theory made much of this. Shakespeare would, in *Macbeth*, flatter James' divine right notions and justify his claim to the throne.

On 24th March 1603, Elizabeth died. The Scottish king quickly posted south, attended by numerous ambitious aristos, hangers-on and the handsome young men he liked to have around him. He would not return for fourteen years. 'For the king,' wrote an English courtier, 'every day will be Christmas.'

No-one much liked James, though his admiration for himself was sincere, and to some degree deserved.

James invented 'Great Britain' to try to
stop Scots'and English brawling about
precedence. Which brings us to 'Scots',
'Scottish' and 'Scotch' problems! The first

He was a survivor and reigned until 1625. He
managed to dismantle the power of the great nobles,
and constrain that of the Kirk. He commissioned the
monumental translation of the Bible (which effectively
ended the career of Court Scots as a literary language)
and prided himself that the government of Scotland
ran smoothly while he signed the papers in London
(he fixed the Parliament by nominating its executive,
'the Lords of the Articles'). He had much more trouble
with the growing English Puritan force at Westminster, and those who had done well out of looting
Spain and disliked his conciliatory policy.

James thought European. He may have encour-
aged his Danish wife Anne – a grand patron of English
culture at perhaps its zenith: Shakespeare, Donne,
Jonson, Inigo Jones, Dowland, Tallis – to revert to
Catholicism, in order to open a dialogue with Catholic
Europe. But his daughter Elizabeth was married to
protestant Prince Frederick of the Palatinate and he
had also favoured his claims on the Kingdom of
Bohemia.

In 1618-22 this produced disaster. The Bohemians
insulted the Catholic Habsburg who was Holy Roman
Emperor. He destroyed them, and the minor German
rulers closed ranks and retaliated. For thirty years,

two are broadly interchangeable: Scots
(of people: Scots Guards) Scottish (of
things: Scottish scenery). Scotch is archaic
but not English.

Germany would be devastated by Protestant and
Catholic armies – good times for Scottish mercenaries sending money back to their wives and child-
ren in their tower houses (still built for defence in
an age where battlements and stout doors made for
good neighbours).

This wasn't the only sort of enterprise on the go.
With limited woodland, the Scots had exploited coal
for centuries, and some Jacobean magnates, like the
Bruces of Culross, whose Palace is conserved by the
National Trust, were industrialists on a grand scale.
Scots fisheries supplied all of north Europe,
Presbyterians being quite in favour of supplying fish
to Catholic Friday diners, though the carrying trade
was in Dutch hands.

Edinburgh, its choc-a-bloc 'lands' and wynds
perched above the Lothian plain, was by far the
largest town, and a hotbed of Presbyterian enthusiasm, hosting Parliament and Assembly and opening
its municipal, Calvinist university in 1583. Elsewhere
Calvinism was variable in impact, and there were
substantial rural areas where it made no impact at
all.

'An' the king lost his heid, puir gentleman. Mebbe it wasna' a very guid heid, but he was sair in need o' it.'

7. Covenant and Commonwealth

1625 to 1660

JAMES, like Elizabeth, was a survivor and knew how to dodge and weave. His son Charles I was moral and cultivated but small in stature and intellect. In the 1630s he tried to rule without Parliament, to make the Anglican church the instrument of royal authority, and then to impose both on the Scots. The result triggered the English Civil War, more recently reinterpreted as 'The War of the Three Kingdoms'.

It started with the Scots clergy and nobility appealing to the Calvinist people in the National Covenant of 1638, signed publicly in the new Greyfriars Kirkyard in Edinburgh. The King attacked but the Scots, aided by soldiers like Alexander Leslie with plenty of experience in the German wars, defeated his army and cut off coal supplies to London by taking Newcastle. The Irish took advantage of this to revolt and in London, Charles had to recall parliament. He intrigued clumsily, betrayed his supporters like Laud and Strafford (who were executed) then counter-attacked. War broke out.

The Scots mobilised again, this time in alliance with Parliament, in the Solemn League and Covenant of 1643, its aim being to impose Presbyterianism on the English. Initially this was successful, but then the brilliant royalist Marquis of Montrose, commanding Highland and Irish troops, paralysed the Scots, while parliamentary offensives flopped in England. This led Oliver Cromwell to create his New Model Army in 1645: a force upholding unprecedented efficiency over religious dogmatism.

The Presbyterians under David Leslie defeated Montrose but went back to the Stewarts: Charles promised what they demanded. But Cromwell's forces captured, tried and executed him in 1649 and when the Scots persevered with Charles II, Cromwell invaded and unexpectedly devastated Leslie's main army at Dunbar. Charles II himself landed at the mouth of the Spey in 1652, gathered the rest of the Scots army, marched to Worcester, and was thrashed there as well.

Cromwell then consolidated his power in Scotland,

European scholars marvelled at the *praefervidium ingenium Scotorum* (amazing ingenuity of the Scots). James Mill wrote an eight-volume *History of India* (1818) without ever visiting.

---

abolished the parliament, and ruled the country directly – and remarkably fairly – by Major-Generals until he died in 1658.

Something remarkable happened in these hectic years. The English political philosopher Thomas Hobbes captured it in his political treatise *Leviathan*, which emphasised the fact that sovereign power, based in the last analysis on military force and not contract, governed social relations. So much for Presbyterian notions of 'federal Calvinism' or Covenants! In coming international confrontations, *force majeure* and the English notion of 'Crown Imperial' would win out over the Scottish idea of the 'Godly Commonwealth', and circumstances would force many Scots to embrace this destiny.

Not least in still-Catholic Ireland where Stewart monarch and Protector alike found it advantageous to 'plant' former Protestant rebels, many from the Border districts (given to cattle thieving and family conflicts), to hold down the natives recently conquered in Ulster – storing up much trouble for later centuries.

Darien – right place, 200 years too soon

8. Glorious Revolution, Deadly Decade

1660 to 1698

CROMWELL'S RULE in Scotland was, like earlier attempts to control the place, punitively expensive. The Commonwealth ended in 1660 when the General commanding, George Monck, lost patience with Cromwell's incompetent son Richard and marched on London. The restored Charles II, intelligent, cultivated, promiscuous and untrustworthy, knew Scotland and disliked it intensely. He restored the parliament but ordered it about through a trusted Governor, first the Earl of Lauderdale and then his Catholic brother, James, Duke of York.

Like his grandfather, Charles was determined to bring bishops into the Kirk to supervise the Presbyterians, the unruliest of whom styled themselves the true Covenanters and smouldered in the south-west. Brutal guerrilla attacks and repression ensued, recorded by Presbyterians like the Reverend

To some in Scotland, William III is still the
most famous horseman ever, the centre of
the Orange Order whose ultra-Protestant
parades every July keep the seventeenth

Robert Wodrow and the creators of monuments to
the martyrs, still to be found in lonely Galloway glens.

Attempts by the tactless Duke of York to impose
his own ideas on Edinburgh society also caused
rebellions by the lawyers and academics of the town,
and the emergence of a proto-nationalist in the shape
of the soldier and political philosopher Andrew
Fletcher of Saltoun, who joined (and whose fiery
temper disrupted) the fruitless Monmouth rebellion
against James, now king, in 1685. Fletcher represented the old Scots idea of an elective monarchy,
but also the notion of a decentralised, non-imperial
Britain. Circumstances were to force him into a
minority.

The initiative to get rid of James came from
England, not from Scotland. The Whig nobility
appealed in 1688 to his brother-in-law Prince William
of Orange, *Statthalter* of the Netherlands, to displace
him, and William landed at Torbay in Devon. Too
incompetent to raise any sort of counterforce in
Scotland, James fled from London to France. A
Highland rising on his behalf petered out after its
leader James Claverhouse, scourge of the Covenanters and now Viscount Dundee, was killed at Killie-
krankie in 1689, and his campaign in Ireland ended

century alive. Historians point out that at the
Battle of the Boyne, 1 July 1690, Pope
Alexander VIII supported William, but
Scottish sectarianism is beyond history.

with defeat at the Boyne, 1 July 1690. Kirk and
Parliament rejoiced in a specifically Scottish Glorious
Revolution and the return of their liberties after more
than a century of constriction, with the abolition of
the hated Bishops and of the Lords of the Articles.

Then things started to go wrong. In February 1692
the massacre of the MacDonalds of Glencoe discred-
ited the new government. An intense cold spell hit
Scotland, its north European trading partners, and
famines struck in 1693-8. Thousands died, and
poverty grew.

In an attempt to break out, a bold speculator
William Paterson, founder of the Bank of England in
1694, organised the Bank of Scotland and the
'Company of Scotland trading to the Indies' in 1695.
New Edinburgh would rise on the isthmus (neck of
land) of Darien in Central America, over which a new
road would link the Atlantic and Pacific.

Two thousand colonists were sent out, in two
expeditions, but England and Spain combined to
isolate the Scots. New Edinburgh proved a fever-pit.
Only about 300 eventually returned (Paterson,
remarkably enough, among them) to a country financ-
ially ruined by the enterprise.

PART II
IMPERIAL PARTNER

"There is no European nation, which within the course of half a century, or little more, has undergone so complete a change as this Kingdom of Scotland. . . But the change, though steadily and rapidly progressive, has, nevertheless, been gradual; and like those who drift down the stream of a deep and smooth river, we are not aware of the progress we have made until we fix our eye on the now distant point from which we have drifted. . . "

Sir Walter Scott, *Waverley*, 1814

Rogues, parcelling out a nation?
'Every man full of his own merit, and afraid of everyone
near him.' Daniel Defoe

9. Union

1698 to 1715

ALL THIS TIME, the might of France had been increasing, directed by Louis XIV and his ministers. France, in its unified state, had 21.5 million people, Great Britain, under 10 million. At this time Ireland, its Catholics crushed after the campaigns of 1688-90, was fairly quiescent, but Scotland was not. There was the risk that it would resume an independent foreign policy, fuelled by the resentments generated by the Darien failure, and offer France a way in by the back door.

On the other hand, Darien left many like Paterson believing that formal parliamentary union with England was the best way out. It wasn't as if the Parliament offered all that much to the Scots. Its electorate was tiny, compared to that of England: a few score freeholders in each county, and town councils who nominated their own successors. Perhaps 4500 voters in all, out of a population of over a million.

There were alternatives. The Kirk had its General

Whig comes from 'Whiggamore!' a call of Scottish
cattle-drovers in the 17th century, but Whigs were as
grand as German princes. Tory referred to Irish

Assembly, meeting every year for three weeks, in
charge of poor relief and education, and general social
discipline. The four universities were independent,
and lawyers had their own governing body in the
Faculty of Advocates. The towns had the Convention
of Royal Burghs, which also controlled overseas
economic policy. Parliament, under the Lords of the
Articles, hadn't been allowed to interfere with any of
these. Should it now be allowed to do so?

One group which had too much autonomy was the
nobility, who had thrived as the monarchy had
declined. The Douglas Dukes of Hamilton and the
Campbell Dukes of Argyll possessed 'heritable
jurisdictions', monarch-like privileges which could
not be brought under the control of London ministers. Since it was evident that Queen Anne, daughter
of William and Mary, was unlikely to produce an heir,
attention focused on the next in line, the Elector of
Hanover, descended from James I's daughter Elizabeth, the Winter Queen of Bohemia.

So the Scottish MPs and more importantly the
noblemen who sat with them in the parliament, had
to be brought to London, by 'stuffing their mouths
with gold', and ensuring that the Commissioners who
were to negotiate the Treaty were pliable.

Catholic outlaws, on account of Jacobite links. Whigs 'died out' with the rise of liberal party organisation in the 1880s. Tories just about continue.

This itself wouldn't have been sufficient. What mattered to the non-noble elites, the burgesses, the lawyers and the Kirk, was that their positions would be guaranteed. It was obvious that they would have to be won over: by compensation for the Darien losses, by subsidies to the linen industry and to coastal fishing. Significantly, the economic clauses of the Treaty were passed by greater majorities than the other parts.

There was, in fact, little enthusiasm for the Treaty of Union on either the Scots or the English side. It was quickly betrayed as a fundamental law (as the Scots liked to think of it) when the Scottish Privy Council was abolished in 1711, followed by a Patronage Act in 1712 which subjected the Kirk to the control of the local 'heritors' or principal landowners. The Treaty was nearly revoked by the Westminster parliament after less than a decade.

What it did imply, however, were important alterations in London politics. It was a significant strengthening of the Commons, and whoever managed them, over the Lords and of Parliament over the Court, something which underlay the long rule of Sir Robert Walpole, Britain's first effective Prime Minister, and his Scottish henchman Alexander Campbell, Duke of Argyll.

Charles Edward Stewart: Say 'Throne of Britain';
don't say 'Tin of Shortbread'

10. A Cause Lost Forever

1715 to 1759

THE TREATY OF UNION accepted in Edinburgh on 17th January 1707 effectively made the 45 surviving Scottish MPs and 16 peers (elected by a pre-Union total of 170) into a commodity, to be purchased by the English rulers. In return, Scottish elites were allowed a great deal of autonomy in their own domestic affairs, lubricated by plenty of patronage.

By the 1720s this was beginning to take effect. Through a combination of legal and illegal enterprise, the ports and merchants of western Scotland established a powerful position in the tobacco and later sugar trades. The Duke of Argyll's power, however, remained a Highland factor, chiefly because London worried about the threat coming from that region.

When Queen Anne died in 1715, and 'the wee, wee German lairdie' Elector George of Hanover succeeded, Lord Mar started a rebellion in the north, which got as far as the inconclusive field of Sherrifmuir near Stirling, and then dispersed. In 1719 a

One of the few women known to Scottish history, Flora MacDonald, concealed Charles Edward and helped him escape to France.

Jacobite army sailed into the River Forth on French ships, but couldn't land. The government's General George Wade laid out a network of military roads, 1725-37, to inhibit another attack.

Then in July 1745, 25 year old Charles Edward Stewart, son of the Pretender James VIII and III, landed at Lochailort, rallied Catholic and Episcopalian clans, and marched on Edinburgh (ironically along Wade's roads). He defeated a Hanoverian force just outside the city and commandeered Holyrood Palace (though the Castle held out against him) then headed south. His Highlanders got to within 100 miles of London, reaching Derby, then turned back.

Had a French army attacked Dover, things might have been different, but the Highlanders wanted to return home for seed-time, and Charles' army threatened to melt away. He still managed to defeat another Hanoverian force at Falkirk before being pinned down and destroyed at Culloden on 16th April 1746. He made his escape through the Hebrides. Despite a rich reward offered by the government, no clansman betrayed him.

But the traditional military tenures of the clans

He died of drink in 1788; she became one of the 'Empire Loyalists' who left the new USA for Canada in 1783.

were now suppressed and the chiefs with their legal privileges converted into orthodox landowners. This was an experiment considered so risky that the government had to secure its defences, with one of Europe's greatest fortresses built only a few miles from Culloden at Fort George, 1747-69.

This was what 'civilisation' literally meant: the replacement of 'military tenures' by the rule of state power and civil law. In practical terms, this meant the canny management of Scotland after the 1760s by the Dundas family of Edinburgh lawyers.

The 1745 rebellion was disastrous for the Jacobite cause, yet by incorporating the Highlanders in the British Army the London government provided itself with a powerful weapon with which to extend its imperial involvement. Almost certainly, as a sixth of her forces, they turned the Seven Years' War of 1753-9 in Britain's favour, in Canada and India. The cause that was lost was that of the people of the Highlands, ill-led by the old order, and exploited by the new.

'These are my mountains,/ And these are my glens'
The Countess of Sutherland improving the Highlands

11. Improvement

1745 to 1900

MORE SCOTS fought for George II at Culloden than fought for the Pretender. The country was already beginning to modernise and urbanise with great speed, and the rebellion was cited to intensify this change, by arguing that without it, disorder would reign. The result was dynamic but scarcely democratic, and carried in its wake a quite conscious propaganda manipulated by those who benefited by it.

The old system of communal farming by townships was 'enclosed' in favour of 'muckle fermers' (large tenants paying high rents for mixed farms) using systems of rotation, horse-ploughs, steadings to house their work-force, high-skilled though ill-paid. About a tenth of Scottish villages were totally rebuilt so that underemployed labourers could spin and weave or fish as well as work on the land. Such settlements were rapidly connected up with turnpike roads, canals were driven from Forth to Clyde and down the Great Glen, and horse-drawn railways linked mines and quarries with waterways.

1822 was a strange year for the Scottish Highlands. King George IV wore the kilt over flesh-coloured tights in Holyrood; the modern whisky

A doctrine of education, social mobility and free markets, which would be codified in Adam Smith's *Wealth of Nations* (1776) was coupled with extensive social engineering. Any energies that might have confounded this were diverted to extending the British Empire. The process would be recorded in the 1790s, parish by parish, in the *Statistical Account of Scotland* organised by the great Caithness landlord Sir John Sinclair, and the exercise was repeated in the 1840s: a sixty-odd volume documentation unique in Europe.

On the basis of the *Statistical Account* the novelist John Galt wrote two 'theoretical histories' in 1821-22, *Annals of the Parish* and *The Provost* which made the whole process seem inevitable. At the time it was known as 'improvement', though some were more conscious of this than others. But it was notable that its opponents themselves seemed to accept that they were marginal forces: secessionists vainly trying to withstand the impersonal forces of 'progress'.

A middle class rose rapidly by turning most social relationships into forms of realisable capital. It created a cultural superstructure that made this tolerable to the masses whose lives were changed,

distillery industry began; and kelp or seaweed harvesting, which kept much of the economy going, started a swift collapse.

though little improved by it. In the 1880s, Arnold Toynbee coined 'the industrial revolution' and in the 1890s came Professor W R Scott's 'The Enlightenment in Scotland'. Both described a highly conscious episode of modernisation.

The first motor of industrial change was the linen industry, traditionally the product of local flaxgrowers and handloom weavers. Innovations in bleaching – from sour milk to sulphuric acid – were brought in, and a market created in the slave-worked plantations of the West Indies and American colonies. By the end of the century, slave-picked cotton was being spun on a far-larger scale in water-powered mills, some of them huge and built in the Scots lowlands. The most famous was New Lanark, built by David Dale in 1785 and passed to his son-in-law Robert Owen. Investment in these and the infrastructure that sustained them came from squeezing wages in favour of middle-class capital for investment in labour-saving equipment, turnpike roads and canals. Scots engineers were outstanding examples of a revolution in technology, involving the use of iron parts such as wheels, rails and beams (stronger than wood and of course fireproof), bricks, and machinecut stone.

When in the 'Great Tea Race' the clipper 'Taeping'
beat the 'Ariel' by 20 minutes sailing from Foochow
(near Hong Kong) to the Pool of London in 1866,
99 days to cover 16,000 miles, the first was owned,

The most famous of Scots inventions was the
steam engine, or rather James Watt's perfecting of
the crude and huge 'atmospheric' mine-pump of
Thomas Newcomen into an efficient supplier of rotary
motion which could pump out mines, haul wagons
and lifts full of coal, or power textile machinery. Watt's
patent dated from 1769, and his engines were built
in Birmingham; hardly twenty of them were actually
in use in Scotland by 1800.

But by 1805, steam engines were applied to water
transport by William Symington, on his *Charlotte
Dundas* tugboat on the Forth and Clyde Canal, and
in 1812 Henry Bell's *Comet* took to the Clyde with
fare-paying passengers.

Such improvements also helped open up the huge
Monklands coal- and iron-field, east of Glasgow, in
the 1820s. This delivered a very pure iron for cast-
ings, just as the market boomed with the first high-
performance locomotive-worked railways. Scotland's
first, the Garnkirk and Glasgow, opened in 1831,
only a year after George and Robert Stephenson's
Liverpool and Manchester. Within eighteen years,
trains ran by the east and west coast routes to London
and as far north as Aberdeen.

Thomas Cook started his cheap excursions in

the second skippered by Anstruther men. In 1884
Sir Sandford Fleming, another Fifer, engineer to the
Canadian Pacific, got international sanction to
divide the world into 24 time zones.

1841. His first shot at Scotland was a failure, but by
1851 he had conveyed Scots of all social classes to
the Crystal Palace in London's Hyde Park, and his
tours became a fixture from Abbotsford to Zetland.
For the Scottish pioneer of industrial history, Samuel
Smiles, the long 'specials' crossing the Royal Border
Bridge at Berwick celebrated the Union.

This was the prelude to an astonishing half-century
in which the Clyde basin literally became the
workshop of the world: its greatest single concentration of locomotive- and ship-building and general
engineering, whose triumphs ran from the Forth
Bridge and Vienna's Prater Wheel to Cunard's
Aquitania and *Queen Mary*. These were essentially
based on a fusion of scientific knowledge and
engineering skills in the 1850s which revolutionised
the marine steam engine from a low-pressure
monster to a high-pressure multi-cylinder power-
pack, and brought the age of sail to an end by 1900.

In turn these brought businesses which mechan-
ised former handcrafts and service industries, like
Europe's biggest factory churning out Singer sewing
machines at Clydebank, Nairn's linoleum factory at
Kirkcaldy, the hardware of the book trade, from
papermaking to binding, or the numerous distilleries
which provided the quickest way out.

'I'd rather be the cause o' one,
than be the death of twenty.'
Robert Burns on morality

12. Ploughmen Poets: Cities of Intellect

1603 to 1832

THE *STATISTICAL ACCOUNTS* showed a country of high literacy. This would be reinforced in every small town by a library and later a newspaper, and many literary and historical clubs and societies. Edinburgh and Glasgow went further and became major centres of publishing.

Scotland was a land of poets in the late middle ages: enough for the Calvinists of 1560 to appeal to the ordinary folk with their *Gude and Godlie Ballads*: rapping for the reformation! Thereafter the Kirk's hostility to theatre and dance clamped down, and talent would mainly be found on the cavalier side: the 'Castalian Band' of poets around James VI and during the Civil War, the Marquess of Montrose and the extraordinary Sir Thomas Urquhart of Cromarty. Alternatively, there were the Border Ballads with their mixture of violence, vamping until ready, and heartbreaking beauty:

But I hae dreamed a dreary dream
Ayont the isle o' Skye.
I saw a dead man win a fight
And knew that man was I.

Covenanters had legends of persecution and resistance which looked like a proto-Western, and John Bunyan's *Pilgrim's Progress* (1776) soon found itself on every cottar's shelf. Early in the eighteenth century Allan Ramsay, an Edinburgh printer, collected folk songs and wrote a Jacobite drama, *The Gentle Shepherd* (1725), which villagers staged for over a century.

The next episode was remarkable. In 1760-3, schoolteacher James MacPherson claimed to have detected old Gaelic manuscripts on an epic scale. *Ossian* was a phenomenon of the *Lord of the Rings* sort and, many argued, a complete fake. On the other hand it influenced a whole generation of early romantics, notably Goethe, Napoleon and (most influential in the long term) the German Johann Gottfried Herder, who made the fateful link between language, culture and nationality.

MacPherson died a rich man; so too did Henry Mackenzie, the author of the tear-jerking *Man of Feeling* (1771). Both have long fallen from fashion, but the 'sympathy' they set out to conjure up was taken seriously, notably by Adam Smith, who had started off his career as a lecturer on literature.

Much more positive was to come. Robert Fergusson, a young Edinburgh lawyer, revived Dunbar's bawdy, affectionate treatment of the capital in the 1760s, and in 1786 came *Poems, chiefly in the Scottish Dialect* by an unknown young farmer, Robert Burns. Burns was first a success, then a cult. Perhaps only now are the Scots coming to terms with his genius as a poet of the love and patriotism he knew, and the equality and democracy that he foresaw. The son of an unsuccessful small farmer, he was exceptionally well educated. His reading was that of an enlightened citizen – Adam Smith, David Hume and James Thomson – and his politics were radical, sympathising with the American and French revolutions:

> *From scenes like these,*
> *old Scotia's grandeur springs,*
> *That makes her lov'd at home, rever'd abroad*
> *Princes and lords*
> *are but the breath of kings,*
> *An honest man's the noblest work of God.*

His enjoyment of love – idealistic and erotic – was unqualified.

Yestreen when to the trembling string
The dance gaed thro' the lighted ha'
To thee my fancy took its wing,
I sat, but neither heard nor saw:
Tho' this was fair, and that was braw,
And yon the toast of a' the town,
I sigh'd, and said amang them a',
Ye are na Mary Morison.

As George Orwell noted, this is poetry that pierces the heart.

Burns met, at Professor Adam Ferguson's house in Edinburgh, a polite and knowledgeable boy with a limp. This was the young Walter Scott, born in Edinburgh to a lawyer's family but brought up in the Borders, with its strong oral culture and the recent memory of invasion by English and Jacobites. Scott first made his name as a folklorist, then as a writer of narrative verse like *Marmion*, and after 1814 as a novelist with *Waverley*, the story of a young and ingenuous Englishman, caught up in the 1745 rebellion and torn between the two sides. The author of *Waverley* remained officially anonymous for another score of books. He was a Tory and had Jacobite emotions, but was otherwise an 'improving' businessman – gas company and railway director – brought down in 1826 by his speculations in publishing.

Other talents included the 'Ettrick Shepherd' James Hogg, illiterate until his teens, then the writer of brilliant parodies and satires, and the dark and disturbing *Confessions of a Justified Sinner* (1822). John Galt, in *Annals of the Parish* and *The Provost* marshalled the facts of the *Statistical Accounts* into a panorama of the shift from agriculture to new industry – and the New World.

What happened in Scotland was projected by literary men – and some women like Susan Ferrier or Margaret Oliphant – worldwide. They underwrote the popular enlightenment of the nineteenth century – adult education, medical reform, civic universities, cheap publishing. Some Englishmen mocked; more took advantage of it and muscled in.

By the end of the nineteenth century nearly half the Scottish population lived in the four main cities of Glasgow (one million), Edinburgh (450,000), Aberdeen (200,000) and Dundee (200,000). About 75% lived in urban areas, while in the country, numbers which had increased steeply until the 1870s, now fell with the downturn in the agricultural economy after cheap grain and meat could be imported.

Scientific intellect had been important for the Scots. In the seventeenth century it led the ambitious

> Patrick Geddes, 1856-1932, had the gift of
> thinking brilliant thoughts just as a guilt-
> ridden millionaire happened by.

to careers in the army or to attend institutions like
Leiden University in the Netherlands. Back home
there were the Edinburgh clubs and publishers and
increasingly art dealers such as the Foulis brothers
of Glasgow, who created a taste for the classical
among the city's middle classes. The *Encyclopaedia
Britannica*, modelled on that of Diderot in Paris
(1751), began in Edinburgh in 1769.

The regional intellect in Aberdeen was influenced
by the agri-capitalism of Buchan and the dealings of
the herring fishery, the common sense philosophy of
Thomas Reid and plentiful bursaries which meant
'Buchan loons and quines' becoming teachers throughout the country in the new Board Schools of 1872.

Dundee first rose with coarse linens, then with
whaling. Whale oil aided the astonishing rise of the
jute industry, which provided the packaging for the
international trade Britain dominated, and led to vast
fortunes.

But Glasgow was altogether different in scale. Why?
It was already a major clerical and educational centre
in the Middle Ages, sited at the lowest ford on the
Clyde. In the late seventeenth century it rose on the
Atlantic trade, establishing a deep-water harbour
near Greenock which became Port Glasgow. It was

He got money from Carnegie, was revered
by Nehru, inspired Roosevelt's Tennessee
Valley Authority.

from here, and from ports as far south as Whitehaven in Cumbria (with a lot of smuggling thrown in), that the city flourished on the tobacco trade. By 1776 the city was booming, with the linen trade growing. The Clyde was deepened, a canal from Clyde to Forth projected and partly built, and the centre planned on an American-style gridiron pattern.

The American Revolution hit Glasgow hard, but it bounced back with the next boom, in cotton, which marked the 1780s, and made Clyde cotton second only to that of Lancashire. Moreover, this triggered advances in engineering and finance. The blackband ironstone of the Monklands, first exploited in 1829, completed the takeoff. By 1851 Glasgow's population was 345,000, trebling again by 1911. The downside was that this was achieved at the expense of living standards. High immigration and employment accompanied tiny, congested and unsanitary housing.

'We war with rude nature, and come off always victorious, and loaded with spoils.' Thomas Carlyle

13. Rule Britannia!

1745 to 1914

PATRONAGE was one of the main drivers of the Union. The soldiers from 'cleared' Highland glens fought at the bidding of a generation of younger sons 'on the make', who risked their lives as officers or 'clerks' of the great London chartered companies, and expected rewards to match. Their breakthrough came even earlier than the fighting men, and cemented the dominance of the Scots in expanding the Empire. They had talked an ambitious game. Now they could use their less-fortunate kinsfolk to make the gamble work.

In the eighteenth century the two main areas contested with the French were North America and India. In the first, the Scots built up the trapping and fur business of the Hudson's Bay Company, and then leagued with friendly Red Indian tribes to expel the French. The fall of Quebec in 1759 was critical, and was shortly followed by the expulsion of the French from most of their East Indian territories. This was to the advantage of the likes of James Mill

Small towns and global heroes: Thomas Telford,
master engineer was a shepherd's son from
Westerkirk. His money founded Langholm Library.
Another 'muckle touner' William Mickle translated

and a succession of Scots governors, industrialists and
plantation-owners. Most of the 'nabobs' who survived
(a minority) came back loaded. Gentle Jane Austen
didn't care for people called Crawford or Dalrymple.

The Scot overseas was initially unreassuring.
Darien wasn't unique. In 1722 John Law of Lauriston
nearly destroyed France with his Mississippi Scheme.

To Burns, the Scots aristocrat went off to Europe:

> *To make a tour an' tak a whirl,*
> *To learn bon ton an' see the worl'.*
> *There at Vienna, or Versailles,*
> *He rives his father's auld entails;*
> *Or by Madrid he takes the rout,*
> *To thrum guitars and fecht wi' nowt.*

But he (or his teachers, like David Hume and Adam
Smith) came back with the classic taste that created
both Edinburgh's New Town, and the 'national'
painting of Allan Ramsay Junior, Henry Raeburn and
David Wilkie.

After 1759 expansion was rapid: a mixture of
military victory and trading deals, many on the windy
side of the law. The English elites tended to mirror
the hierarchies of London and the cathedral cities
they were used to; the Irish moved into the big towns,

the Portuguese discovery epic the *Lusiads*.
Christopher Grieve was born in the Library and
read every book. Neil Armstrong, first man on the
moon, got the burgh's freedom in 1972.

where they provided the labour to be managed by
shrewd Scots like John Young, the Ayr-born creator
of the port of Montreal. Scots could also be found on
the land, where the botanic garden – adapting plants
to new habitats – became a major instrument of
imperial expansion. Dock engineering, speculative
suburbs and later on railways like the Canadian
Pacific and urban tramways: the Scots attended to,
and lived from, the institutions of the new colonies.

From the mid-nineteenth century they gained
further prestige from missionary activity, combined
with education in India and African exploration. This
was enough in the hands of Dr David Livingstone to
drown out discussion of the cash brought in by
firewater (whisky loosened up natives for conquest)
and the opium trade for which the British subjugated
the Chinese in the 1840s.

By the 1908-12 depression, emigration was no
longer a wrench or a gamble but a career option.
Two Harvie great-uncles, architect and engineer,
slipped smoothly from Motherwell into the Vancouver
bourgeoisie; there was a class at Edinburgh's Royal
High specially run for the Shanghai Bank.

'From the lone shieling, and the misty island,
Mountains divide us, and a waste of seas.
But still the blood is strong, the heart is highland,
And we in dreams behold the Hebrides'

14. Reform

1832 to 1948

*'People crushed by law have no hopes but
from power. If laws are their enemies, they
will be enemies to laws.'*

THE WORDS were those of a great Liberal and
historian, of Gaelic descent, T B Macaulay.

Britain's was a liberal empire, and much of its
effectiveness came from the free movement of its
elites among the institutions of state.

The 1832 Reform Act wasn't achieved without a
struggle, particularly in English towns, where the
Castle of Nottingham and the Palace of Bristol were
laid low. Scotland was quieter, but her intellectuals,
running the *Edinburgh Review*, had done much to
expand the agitation. The English electorate doubled,
the Scots (extended by creating new urban constituencies) went up from 5000 to 65,000.

Reform, however, did little for the mass of the

Scots shoppers are criticised for encouraging
supermarkets, yet they pioneered mass-
marketing in the nineteenth century with Sir

people. How were they to cope with sheep evicting
them from the glens, and 'muckle fermers' enforcing
flight into the towns? Up to the 1840s this upheaval
seemed almost apocalyptic, and even among the well-
off there thrived millenarian or utopian ideals.

Robert Owen, the owner of the New Lanark Mills
and social experimenter, promoted his 'new view of
society' at every possible opportunity. His schemes
usually collapsed, but they trained a generation of
working-class activists who would eventually gain a
qualified utopia in the Co-op societies.

Chartism was political rather than social; its
leaders, organised on a British basis, argued for their
'six points': universal manhood suffrage, equal
electoral districts, payment of members, secret
ballots, no property qualifications, and annual
parliaments. Scots Chartists were well organised,
generally moral-force and legalistic, and ineffective.
If you wanted to be a democrat, then go to Canada,
or by the 1850s Australia and New Zealand.

By the mid-century there were also civic careers
to be made in the churches, medicine, and education.
Tasks that would, in Europe, have gone to national
parliaments, were shared between Westminster and
increasingly powerful Scottish burghs with elected

Thomas Lipton's chain stores and the branches of the Co-ops, which could take as much as 30% of local commerce.

councils. From 1833, the powers of these councils were expanded to cope with the challenges of poverty, disease and pollution. They were tasks which lay before a country particularly famous for its medical reforms: Simpson and chloroform, Lister and antisepsis, spectacularly boosted by projects like Glasgow's water supply, piped from Loch Katrine in 1859.

'Municipal progress' was also cultural, as Glasgow's Art Gallery testified. Her young painters, the 'Glasgow Boys' and 'Scots Colourists' were an exhilarating change from academic portraits and stags at bay, and their School of Art by Charles Rennie Mackintosh, opened 1899-1910, became one of Europe's most admired buildings.

In 1867 the vote was conceded to urban male householders, and the first sustained campaign for women's suffrage began. Women could soon vote for and sit on local councils and school boards, and gain access to universities and teaching hospitals although their parliamentary vote came only in 1918. The present single-member constituencies date from the Third Reform Act of 1884, but 'one person one vote' came as late as 1948. In 1969 the voting age was dropped from 21 to 18 years. 16 year olds will be able to vote for Scottish independence in 2014.

15. A House Divided

1832 to 1885

THE GREAT PUBLIC debate in Victorian Scotland was not, however, about politics but about religion. The issue of control of the Kirk had throbbed away, parish by parish, in the eighteenth century. But as political reform gained momentum, the religious issue moved alongside it. It had little to do with theology, much more with the Church's prominent social position – far greater than in any other European country – dominating education, poor relief, and social discipline.

To begin with, religious politics had consisted of 'seceding': stalking out of the Kirk while usually still claiming to embody it. But as the evangelical revival gained support (after the 1780s supported by the Dundas family), the struggle returned to the parish. Shortly after the 1832 Act, the 'wild party' under the social reformer the Reverend Thomas Chalmers, got a majority. Not least because of its links with the press, expertly led by Cromarty stonemason, geologist and social thinker, Hugh Miller, editor of *The Witness*.

The Disruption drama was recorded by the artist D. O. Hill and photographer Robert Adamson, making up a huge crowd scene 'The Signing of the Deeds of Demission' from hundreds of individual calotypes. These were superb, the picture almost comic.

After 1834 congregations resisted the 'intrusion' of lairds' nominees; fighting through the Church courts and then, on appeal, to the Court of Session. Westminster Whigs didn't really want to know about the issue, since the Scots were unlike English non-conformists in wanting to retain an established church. The Tories wouldn't move against their aristocratic allies.

In 1842 the Home Secretary Sir James Graham threw the Kirk's 'Claim of Right' out. This provoked a third of the General Assembly in May 1843 to found the Free Church: known thereafter as the Disruption. The result was an obsessive competition to build as many churches as possible. By the 1860s Scots small towns had up to six half-empty gothic barns. The conflict would limp on until Kirk reunion finally came in 1929.

It was probably in this decade that 'North Britain' came closest to describing the place. But even then protests at governmental delays were starting to mount, and the creation of the Scotch Education Department in London in 1872 intensified the call for a Scottish Minister. Fear of the country following Ireland into agrarian revolt forced this concession –

the revival of the Scottish Office under a Scottish Secretary – in 1885.

W. E. Gladstone led the Liberals to offer the Irish home rule a year later. This took until 1921 to gain, with much violence after 1916, when co-leader of the Dublin Rising was James Connolly from Edinburgh. But Gladstone's bill inspired Scots to move in favour of devolution. This mattered as much to Keir Hardie's Scottish Labour Party of 1888 as his socialist objectives.

16. Industry and Empire

1800 to 1914

'A UNION FOR EMPIRE' certainly provided lots of patronage, but this wasn't wholly welcome to Scots 'improvers'. Why? Adam Smith, for one, disapproved of the idea, which he called 'mercantilism', of building up national strength at the expense of other nations – though this described pretty fairly the relations between the states of eighteenth-century Europe.

The fringes of sharp trading practice – smuggling, piracy, downright fraud – were murky, and until late in the eighteenth century colonies were seen as captive markets, rather than as the source of raw materials: something that partly led to the American revolt in 1776.

This was a setback to Scotland the trading nation. The tobacco lords were badly hit. But trade bounced back in the shape of sugar and cotton, provided by the last phase of human slavery in the West Indies and America. Scots were not directly involved in the

Golf probably came to Scotland from
Holland; it reached London in 1603 with
James VI and Calcutta in 1829, before

Africa-to-Caribbean slave trade, centred in Bristol
and then Liverpool, but profited much from supplying the plantations with equipment, and building
machinery to refine their products – spinning-frames,
sugar boilers and so on.

This wasn't yet the world of steam-powered
technology, but it gave birth to it. Think, for instance,
of the Stevenson family, who built the intricate stone
tower lighthouses of the Northern Lights which tamed
the fierce coasts of the Hebrides and the Pentland
Firth. Or of Telford, who saw his projects as 'a great
working academy' and schooled such 'national tech-
nologists' as William Dargan in Ireland, John Eric-
sson in Sweden and the USA and Joseph Mitchell
who built the Highland Railway.

After 1880 there was a scramble for territories
between the European states. Had Scotland still been
independent she might have picked up a few thous-
and square miles of jungle or desert somewhere.
Empire, and the disinclination of English grandees
to have much to do with trade in it, gave the Scots
plenty of scope in places like Montreal, Singapore,
and Hong Kong.

The Scots managed to stay on both sides of the
argument, imposing British rule and exploitation, but

provincial England (1860s) let alone America
(1884). The Royal and Ancient Club codified
the rules in St Andrews in 1853.

often organising the resistance of settlers, or even
natives, against it.

William Lyon MacKenzie headed the campaign for
responsible government in 1830s Canada, Sir John
A. MacDonald was its first Prime Minister in 1867,
Allan Hume founded the Indian Congress in 1885,
Andrew Fisher was the first Labour Prime Minister
of a federal Australia in 1908. By 2000 it was
reckoned that 25 million Scots lived worldwide, small
in comparison with a global population of 6.6 billion,
but exercising disproportionate influence.

Though could an imperial race base itself on a
working-class living in the tiny tenements of Glasgow:
'Second City'? . . . or 'Naples with bad weather'? As
the Liberals swept to their greatest-ever victory in
1906, this question was becoming insistent in the
town planning movement of men like Professor
Patrick Geddes, and the intensifying of the agitation
for women's suffrage.

'. . . and, all unseen, romance brought up the 9.15'
Rudyard Kipling

17. Finest Hour

1914 to 1918

IN 1904 the First Lord of the Admiralty, Lord Cawdor, commissioned a huge new turbine-powered, ten-heavy-gun battleship, HMS *Dreadnought*. In one step this made the 100-odd capital ships of the Royal Navy obsolete and triggered an expensive naval race with Germany. Speed, armour and guns escalated, though overhead and undersea new, far more deadly, weapons waited. Ten years later, the guns started firing.

Britain was dragged into World War I by treaty obligations to protect Belgium, but the conflict came after some years of intense political upheaval in practically every European state – the 1905 revolution in Russia, the Dreyfus Case in France, widespread labour conflicts – and alliances. John Buchan played a major role in propaganda, Sir William Weir in munitions production, while Sir Douglas Haig became British Commander in Chief.

War propaganda was an early success which owed

A lady from hell . . . A poison dwarf . . .
See him, Kamerad, and run . . .

to the Scots involvement in mass literacy, ranging from Buchan's *Thirty-Nine Steps* and Ian Hay's *The First Hundred Thousand* to the apparently powerful documentation of German atrocities in Belgium in the Bryce Committee's report of 1915.

In May 1915 Lloyd George and his business allies, 'men of push and go', tackled the arsenals of Krupp, RheinStahl and Skoda, and won. The Germans don't seem to have believed that Clyde munitions production was possible on the scale achieved. Lloyd George's War Cabinet followed from his munitions success at the end of 1916 and two of its five members were Scots. The margin of their fight was narrow.

Austria and Turkey depended on the 'warfare state' of Germany. Of the allies, the Russian steamroller never got properly moving: a primitive road and rail system, aristocratic incompetence and corruption saw to that. The Germans set out to wear the French away at the fortress of Verdun, inspiring the first great British push to relieve them, at the Somme in 1916 (June to November). A bloodbath, it still showed the power Britain had in reserve.

In early 1917 Tsarist Russia collapsed, and desperate measures were taken to keep the unstable

In Athens in 1918 British Intelligence was
Major Compton Mackenzie; his assistant
was Lieutenant Saunders Lewis. Within a
decade they would found, respectively, the

Russian republic in the war. In vain: French and British offensives ended in terrible slaughter, and there was menace at sea – not from the German fleet, after the drawn battle of Jutland in May 1916 – but from near-lethal, 'unrestricted U-boat warfare'.

Clyde shipyards had to replace the losses, though in April 1917 this brought the USA into the war, just as the Bolsheviks took Russia out. For the period until US troops arrived Britain stood against Germany with, as Haig put it, 'our backs to the wall'.

The army that pressed eastwards from Cambrai, France, in mid-1918 was far different from the tiny force that had landed in Belgium in 1914. Thousands of brand new weapons had been manufactured for it – planes, trucks, tanks, machine-guns, bombs, and millions of tons of high-explosive shells. 'Dilution' of the labour-force enabled this. 30,000 out of 57,000 Clydeside munitions workers were women by 1918, when those over 30 were rewarded with the vote. But this pressure changed and distorted the machinery and methods of the Clyde, making any return to peacetime trade difficult. . .

. . . for those who stayed. The left journalist Lord Ritchie-Calder said of the troops who left his home town of Forfar:

National Party of Scotland (1928) and Plaid Cymru, the Party of Wales (1925). Unknown to them Christopher Grieve was working as a medical orderly in Thessalonika.

'They marched to the station, and they never came back.'

'Were they killed?' asked his son Angus.

'No. they just didn't come back.'

There was also another secretive war to do with promoting nations against empires, where Scotland's cosmopolitanism played its part: with R.W. Seton-Watson among the south Slavs, Arthur Balfour and the Jews, the half-Scots T.E. Lawrence and the Arabs. Lord Bryce tried to help the Armenians, and authored the 'covenant' idea behind the League of Nations. Why not – with Ireland's 1916 rebellion in mind – come closer to home?

Within the two-party system, the war caused an earthquake. In 1906 the Liberals had a near-monopoly of Scots MPs. By 1922 they had been overtaken by Labour, swollen by the 'Red Clyde', growing trade unionism and the wider franchise granted in 1918. After 1939 the party of Gladstone all but disappeared for twenty years.

PART III
CHOOSING A FUTURE

O Scotland is
The barren fig.
Up, carles, up
An' roond it jig.
Old Moses took
A dry stick and
Instantly it
Floo'red in his hand.
Pu' Scotland up,
An' wha can say
It winna bud
An blossom tae!
A miracle's
Oor only chance
Up, carles, up
And let us dance!

Hugh MacDiarmid, 1926

18. Depression and Renaissance

1920 to 1955

UNEMPLOYMENT and emigration branded Scotland during the 1920s: 'that depressed region'. After making good wartime losses, postwar exhaustion kept joblessness around 14%, worsening to 22% in the early 1930s. Roughly 10% of the population left the country for England and – until the catastrophic Wall Street slump of 1929 – overseas.

The heavy industries contracted or were 'rationalised' but generally survived. It was the smaller, locally owned firms making general machinery and consumer goods that went to the wall, carrying much of the country's enterprise culture with them. Many of the radical promises of the Lloyd George government were forgotten, though electrification expanded with the creation of the National Grid, the telephone system grew, and for many families the cinema, particular after the talkies in 1929, replaced the Kirk.

Quite different, and so small-scale in its units of organisation as to come in 'under the radar' was the 'Scottish renaissance' which began in the middle of the 1920s under a remarkable figure: Christopher Grieve, 'Hugh MacDiarmid'. MacDiarmid was a fine lyric poet and critic but possessed of a mission to drag the country on to its feet as a European nation. He was hopeless at party politics but as dramatic as Thomas Carlyle – 'a bolt of lightning in a china shop' – as a mobiliser and cultural liberator. Other writers clustered round him: Eric Linklater, Neil Gunn, Lewis Grassic-Gibbon, Sorley MacLean. Culturally, this investment would pay off in five decades, even if politically the prospects for nationalism looked near hopeless.

> *O wae's me on the weary days*
> *When it is scarce grey licht at noon;*
> *It maun be a' the stupid folk*
> *Diffusin' their dullness roon and roon.*
> *Like soot,*
> *That keeps the sunlicht oot.*
> *Nae wonder if I think I see*
> *A lichter shadow than the neist*
> *I'm fain to cry 'The dawn, the dawn!*
> *I see it brakin' in the East.'*
> *But ah, It's juist mair snaw!*

Was the rise of the Labour party under its Scots leader, Ramsay Macdonald (minority Prime Minister at Westminster in 1924 and 1929), any compensation? A trade union and councillor establishment squeezed out the ethical socialists of the Independent Labour Party (ILP), and the National Party of Scotland was largely a 1928 breakaway from the ILP. Both made little progress, in comparison with the disproportionately Scots-led Communists in the trade unions.

Yet equally fruitless was the General Strike of May 1926, when railwaymen and dockers came out across Scotland to support the miners, whose wages were to be cut. It was well-behaved and unsuccessful, and this diverted the unions from direct action to building up Labour's control of local government. They won Glasgow, Aberdeen and Dundee by 1935, and stayed put until the new century. Socialism meant the takeover of housing through state subsidy and local authority ownership, a policy begun by the ablest of the Clydesiders, John Wheatley, during the brief Labour government of 1924.

A stronger Labour minority regime took office under MacDonald in 1929, only to be hit when the Crash ended the USA's post-war boom. The Cabinet struggled with mounting unemployment, but refused to back expenditure cuts. MacDonald with King George V's support formed a National Government largely of Conservatives, which slaughtered his old party at the 1931 election. He then talked vaguely about devolution.

Most business leaders opposed home rule, but one of them, the Clydeside magnate Sir James Lithgow, helped create such economic institutions as the Scottish National Development Council, incorporated into interventionist government by a remarkable Tory, Walter Elliot.

In fact, with the relaunch of the Scottish National Party (1933) in the background, progressive patriotism had a good decade, unlike elsewhere in Europe where it was seen off by drums and marching men. Rearmament took the edge off the depression after 1935, and Secretary Elliot managed a brief feast of Art Deco with the commissioning of the 'Queen Mary', the 1938 Glasgow Empire Exhibition and St Andrews House, the government HQ in Edinburgh.

Scotland's hour, however, came again with war. As the hinge of Europe and the Atlantic, it was a strategic key. In 1940 it became a base for Norwegian and Polish loyalists, driven into exile by the German

Electrical power generated in Scotland rose from 1900 Megawatt hours (MWh) in 1939 to 3017 in 1961, 10,378 in 1978 and 48,217 in 2007. The

blitzkrieg. From 1941 it hosted the Americans, first with lend-lease aid, then with planes and troops; Prestwick became Europe's busiest airport. After Russia joined the allies, Scottish naval bases and sea lochs were the junctions where convoys were marshalled for the eastern front.

Prime Minister Winston Churchill made an inspired choice in Tom Johnston, his foe as a journalist on the Red Clyde, as Secretary of State. Johnston built up Scotland's transit and supply role, while planning great hydro-electric schemes for the Highlands, carried out between 1945-62. Supporting the Beveridge Report of 1942, he gave bipartisan social reform a strong Scottish accent. But on the whole, the experience of war and the heroic leading role of London, 'Churchill's city', bolstered a British ethos which took a generation to fade.

Clement Attlee and Labour, elected rather surprisingly in 1945 (though its success in Scotland was less sweeping) added to this Britishness with the Welfare State, the National Health Service and the nationalisation of the service industries: coal, electricity and gas, steel, docks, aviation, buses, railways. The Scots were generally grateful, but a bit

watt was named after James Watt. It wasn't being used in manufacturing, 66% of Gross Domestic Product in 1935, 44% in 1976, and 16% in 2009.

breathtaken by the centralisation involved, and there was a large-scale though short-lived nationalist reaction, the Covenant movement, directed by John MacCormick, earlier first Secretary of the SNP (Scottish National Party).

On the rim of all this, on the Isle of Jura, George Orwell wrote a book about how freedom depended on language and history: *1984*. Around him, Gaelic was dying out.

Labour decreed a Festival of Britain for 1951, held in London. Churchill, back with his Tories in that year, had his return match with the Coronation of Elizabeth II in 1953. Balmoral was reborn for the TV age, but the magic didn't last.

Scotland's summers get wetter and wetter – fact.
So, aff tae Tenerife!

19. Administrative Devolution

1945 to 1974

THE AFTERMATH of World War II was, on the surface, far different from the disaster of the 1920s. Because German and Japanese shipyards and engineering works were heaps of rubble, industrial Scotland had a second boom. But little investment was going into the traditional industries, and although there were some attempts at consumer goods (in 1950 Dundee made more clocks than Switzerland) small houses and low incomes still inhibited these. Scotland was stuck back in its own 1900s, not even getting to the English 1930s.

The Empire, though still extensive, was proving impossible to hold. The fall of Singapore in 1942 had been its death sentence; this was carried out when Britain and France attacked the Suez Canal in 1956 to recapture the pivotal imperial link. They were repulsed, not just by Colonel Nasser's Egyptian

---

Only 2% of Scots commuters use Fleming
and Dunlop's energy-efficient safety bike.
They love their cars and spend over £12

---

nationalists, but by John Foster Dulles at the US State
Department.

While Suez was closed, the size of tankers soared,
from 40,000 to over 250,000 tons, far too big to be
built on the Clyde. Shrewd bosses took the hint and
invested in greenfield sites in South Korea. Railways
declined – temporarily – but enough to kill off the
steam-age Glasgow locomotive industry. The Scottish
coalfield, fading away for years in its main centre of
Lanarkshire, faced first hydro-electricity, then
nuclear power. A similar but slower nemesis overtook
textiles, cookers, furniture, porcelain, linoleum and
carpets.

Labour benefited from the political backlash, and
after Harold Wilson's government (1964-70) and its
planning solutions came unstuck (its one real
success, the Open University, was Scots in inspir-
ation) the reviving SNP stood ready.

But Scots commerce found it difficult to compete.
'Would you rather shop at Marks and Sparks or the
Co-op?' was the key question, and the old 'store' with
its 'divvy', lack of credit, and fusty fashions lost out.
The same went for small holiday resorts with dodgy
weather when charter flights to the Mediterranean

billion a year on them, yet attempts at mass-manufacture, from the Argyll to the Hillman Imp, have all ended in failure.

---

started in the mid-1950s. By the 1970s the Scottish high street looked like anywhere else in the UK, but its people's politics were different. In 1955 the Tories with 50% support, had been top party; after 1959 Scotland was their weakest link.

Deindustrialisation brought resistance, and an attempt in 1971 by the incoming Heath government to close most Clyde shipyards was met by a 'work-in' at the John Brown shipyard led by the remarkable duo of Jimmy Reid and Jimmy Airlie. Shrewd as well as brave, this saved equipment and skills to tackle the oil opportunity. Scots didn't much fancy entry to what became the European Union in 1975, though they voted for it. Later, Europe became popular, because someone down south didn't like it at all. My enemy's enemy is my friend!

'Swing, handbag, swing!'
North Sea oil bankrolls Margaret Thatcher

20. Black Oil, Iron Lady

1979 to 1997

OIL WAS FOUND in 1969 in the Montrose field 100 miles off Aberdeen. Discoveries multiplied and in 1978 the 'black stuff' was being pumped ashore. At its highest, oil made up 4% of UK Gross National Product (GNP) in 1986, and it had a second peak in 1999. The Norwegians had nationalised production in 1971 with Statoil, and by 2007 their GNP per capita was more than $90,000. Scotland's was about half that, which would not have surprised the SNP, who had made a new politics out of the new resource, and in 1974 looked like winning.

Yet they were outwitted by the Labour Party, which promised devolution *and* an oil fund but in fact shrewdly divided the Scots. A devolution bill was laboriously put through Westminster by James Callaghan and John Smith, but failed at a referendum in 1979.

Three months later Mrs Thatcher took power, and was Prime Minisiter of Great Britain until 1990. In a sort of black farce, the oil-propelled petropound shot

TV's principle goes back to Clerk Maxwell's experiments in 1860s. First demonstrated by John Logie Baird in 1925, two years after John Reith's BBC, TV reached Scotland in 1952, 'saturating'

up to nearly $40 a barrel, driven further by the first Iran-Iraq Gulf War and monetarism's high interest rates. This priced UK exports out of world markets, and chopped 20% of Scottish manufacturing.

In Scotland, Thatcher was hated, and not just by her opponents. 'That bloody woman' or 'TBW' as Scots Tories referred to her, destroyed her own party. Their MPs, 26 out of 73 in 1979, fell to 22 in 1983 and to 10 in 1987. Her Scottish Secretary George Younger cleverly manoeuvred to keep many Scots interest groups happy, by fighting to keep the Royal Bank Scots and for the Scottish steel industry, for example, while both Labour and the SNP were convulsed with internal strife.

But subsidies to housing were cut, much of the stock sold off to 'upwardly-mobile' tenants, and the proportion of Scots living in poverty rose from 10% to 25% of the population. Drug use soared in areas traumatised by factory closures, and inept decision-making led to an increase of HIV infection. Irvine Welsh and Danny Boyle marketed this as Scottish urban gothic in *Trainspotting*, book and 1996 film. If you were a man in the most-depressed ward in Glasgow, Calton, you would on average die before age 60.

Scots homes by 1970. Alexander Graham Bell's
telephone came in UK-wide in the 1880s, but
there was only one phone per 10 Scots in 1963;
'saturation' came after 1990.

The bright spots in the economy were two. The
first would prove transient: 'Silicon Glen', a swathe
of hi-tech manufacturing, by the late 1980s extended
from Ayr to Aberdeen. It grew fast but was concentrated on 'screwdriver' manufacturing of hardware –
– mobile phones, computers, printers – which could
easily be transferred elsewhere if works had to be
re-equipped or the labour force grew stroppy.

The Irish concentrated on pharmaceuticals and
software, and prospered: about two-thirds as wealthy
as the Scots in the 1970s, by 2000 they were better
off. By then, little of Silicon Glen remained but the
shiny shells of empty factories. In financial services,
Edinburgh built on its rescued Royal Bank and made
huge sums out of Thatcher's and John Major's privat-
isations and the mortgage boom after the council
house sell-off. Banking expertise helped Scottish
entrepreneurs such as Brian Souter of Stagecoach
and Moir Lockhead of First to make fortunes out of
bus and rail privatisation.

The Scots voters got their act together and voted
tactically to put Conservatives out. After the 1987
election they had only 10 MPs. Then Labour and the
Liberals backed a Constitutional Convention to plan
an agreed scheme of self-government. It first met in

1989 and was steered by its Convenor, the Reverend Canon Kenyon Wright, into producing a report which championed devolution, which most Labourites wanted, and proportional representation for the new parliament, an old LibDem cause. The era of two-party dominance was doomed.

The churches whom Canon Wright represented were already there. They still had record numbers of adherents in the 1960s, but thereafter declined rapidly. The Protestants were first to tumble, but were soon followed by the Catholics. Neither church had taken women seriously, although traditionally it had been women who had held congregations together. Now they had more interesting things to do – education, careers – and left the church in droves.

21. Strands of
Molten Cheese

1997 to 2010

IN MAY 1997 the last Scots Tory MPs were wiped
out. In a September referendum the Scots voted
for devolution by 74% to 26%. Labour politicians
believed that this concession would 'kill nationalism
stone dead', yet after a wobbly start (1999-2004), its
leader Alex Salmond formed a minority SNP government in 2007 and took a majority in 2011.
Independence sentiment fluctuated but could reach
40%, close behind support for devolution. Why?

Two Lib-Lab coalitions 1999-2003 (under Donald
Dewar, Henry McLeish and Jack McConnell) and
2003-2007 (under McConnell) had not tackled the
country's underlying problems: high levels of 'real'
unemployment and consequent poverty, the
expansion of 'jobs for the boys' micro-management,
the stagnation of the small and medium enterprise
(SME) sector.

There was much anger at Labour's foreign policy – the war in Iraq, the new Trident nuclear–weapons – and at oil revenues being used to fund an artificial UK prosperity, based on speculation in real estate and retailing. Meanwhile long-term investment in renewable energy and essential infrastructure, sustainable housing and public transport, was neglected.

In May 2007 the SNP (47 seats) gained from the Scottish Socialists and the Greens, who fell from 13 to two MSPs. Labour still held 46 seats, but lost heavily through the introduction of proportional representation (PR) to local government. (Scotland now had *four* different voting systems for European, Holyrood, local and Westminster elections.) Labour had majorities only in Glasgow and North Lanark. Liberals and Conservatives made no progress.

The SNP leader, Alex Salmond, ran a powerful propaganda campaign, backed by prominent businessmen, notably Sir George Mathewson of the Royal Bank and Brian Souter of Stagecoach, while still offering a social-democrat agenda. His 'minority government' move calculated that by seizing the machinery of power, he could consolidate the SNP advantage. Labour's Tony Blair and later Gordon

Brown obliged by sulking in London (communications with Whitehall were minimal, though good with the devolved governments in Belfast and Cardiff).

Coalitions usually compromise on spending policies – simplifying 'who cut what?' problems – but a minority government doesn't have this excuse. Moreover Whitehall's Consolidated Spending Review was severe. The SNP's actions were populist – freezing local taxes, granting rates rebates to small businesses, ending tolls on road bridges. This was paid for by reducing the budgets of Scottish Enterprise, widely regarded as inefficient, and devolving much administration to local authorities in an 'historic concordat'. Although there was controversy over details, the government's openness was welcomed.

Even in summer 2007, strange writing was on the wall. What *were* SIVs, CDOs, CDOs-squared? Scots savers were as clueless as Chancellor Brown when the tsunami of 'lighter-than air' financial services made the City of London open house for speculators. Douce Edinburgh saw its main banks – the Royal Bank and Halifax Bank of Scotland – in crisis. Savings rates fell from 5% to near zero.

In August 2010 David Cameron announced
that welfare and tax credit fraud and error (by
the unemployed/unfit) cost the taxpayer
£5.2bn a year. 'That's the cost of more than
200 secondary schools or over 150,000
nurses.' In June 2006 leaked Treasury papers

UK investment in 'sub-prime securities' (basically, loaning money to Homer Simpson) seemed to rival the hysteria of John Law's exploits in the 1720s and in the autumn of 2008 it ran out of road. Other small European countries had used their banks to man-oeuvre internationally for independence: Salmond likewise. But after autumn 2008 where *were* the Scottish banks?

310 years on, 'Scotland's pinstripe Darien' brought the country to earth with a terrible bump. The RBS and HBOS were dragged south and much of the Edinburgh financial centre followed them. Credit was tightened for small firms, the last locally-owned manufacturers came under threat. In 2007 the jour-nalist Andrew Marr had written of the Union resem-bling a pizza with a slice being slowly removed until all that held it together were 'strands of molten cheese'. Yet in the May 2010 Westminster election, which saw Gordon Brown on the ropes yet no great enthusiasm outside the English south for the Conservative David Cameron, *nothing in Scotland changed*. Seat by seat, the result was the same as 2005.

revealed that the government estimated an
annual loss of between £97 bn and £157 bn
to tax theft (by the wealthy). This represented
8% to 12% of UK GDP, or the total value of
Scotland's output. (BBC, 9/8/2010; Adam
Taylor, *Guardian*, 10/1/2007)

Things thrived that Holyrood didn't want: the
bonuses of a banking system saved by the taxpayer
but driven by greed and complicity in 'moral hazard'
which had run out of control. Would Cameron's cuts
hit the gentry in their big houses and 4x4s who were
in but not of the countryside? Dream on . . .

Other big cars contained drug barons whose trade
blighted Scots housing estates, its recycled cash
propelling a 'rest and recreation economy' which was
probably bigger than Small and Medium Sized Enterprise (SME) manufacturing. Supermarkets siphon-
ed prosperity out of small towns, and into the vacuum
came tanning, and nail and tattoo parlours,
takeaways and night clubs, whose ownership was
often obscure.

Alcohol, whose real price fell 50% over this period,
joined increasing consumption of fast food from
takeaways, so that by 2010 about 60% were living
unhealthily. 'Sportswear' – among drivers or telly-
addicts – had the Scots catching up on the Americans
in the Sumo stakes. And was 'Jockney' enticing? A
style not a dialect (fewer wrote with accuracy in a
verbal, not a literate, age), too often using the f-word

as noun, verb, adjective, adverb, conjunction, preposition and exclamation.

But this was only part of the story. Crime was falling and (to the degree this could be measured) people were living happier and more fulfilled lives, looking after the old, the chronically ill and the handicapped, contributing generously to charities, conserving the environment. Against this were 'muliply-deprived' inner city areas like Glasgow Calton where drugs, poor diet, alcohol and crime gave a life expectancy of 54 years against Glasgow's 69 and Scotland's 78. Among the fortunate middle class, 'baby boomers' born between 1945 and 1965, missions and settlements, and political work gave way to foreign holidays and second homes. This was in a society where people were more mobile anyway, and different life-stages might involve different environments, but for younger people, especially after the crash of 2008, the keynote was insecurity.

In 2010 ideas about ways forward seemed divergent, but not straightforward. Towards independence? Certainly Scotland was less and less steered by British institutions, many factories and utilities being foreign-owned. Buying into the Great Power game meant a huge cost in arms. Or did the great chance lie in the seas which had surged round the place since the last ice age, the swells that rolled in from the Atlantic, the currents of the Minches and the Pentland Firth? Windfarms, on- and off-shore, were only an overture: tidal and current-driven turbines could provide over 20% of the energy needs of a Europe facing peak oil at around $200 a barrel. In 2012 it was already over $110 and to be masters of this, the Scots needed to assess priorities and invest wisely. The adaptation would not be a comfortable business – it's difficult to re-invent and retrain – but they had no other chance.

Minority government took its toll of the first Salmond Parliament, where only consensus innovations became law. In the May 2012 local elections, Labour clawed back some power. But the Conservative-Liberal Democrat Coalition in London had only 11 LDs and one Conservative in Scotland. Perhaps this put fresh heart into the SNP, because in 2011 they fought a model campaign and won 69 out of 129 MSPs: the first Scottish Government with an overall majority.

22. 'Stands Scotland where it did?'

. . . asks MacDuff in *Macbeth*, and gets a pile of vocal grievances dropped on him. Not easy to generalise about, identity in Scotland has always operated at several levels, between family and empire. A nation of five ethnic groups, yet unified by the eleventh century, it came in with a top-heavy, privileged political-religious class, whose talents were exportable – to Scandinavia and France as well as (up to 1300) England. Anglo-Scottish confrontation up to 1560 was exceptional rather than the norm. It couldn't really function after England seized sea-power. This both required and fostered integration within the islands, though not English dominance.

The consequence was that links and arguments were open – both between the Scottish 'estates' and between the two countries – even when contradictions were seen from outside. The Parliaments (and the nobles) were always rivalled by the Kirk, especially after 1707, and within the elite by the Advocates, the Universities, the Burghs. Scots traded with the Veere staple despite England's wars. The balance changed after the 1745 rebellion: the military society of the Highlands adopted political goals, also shifting from Europe to the empire.

Thomas Carlyle's 'gospel of work', seemingly non-national, also implied a dismissal of English deference as servility. The 'raucle tung' of the Doric had its own strong discourse, from Burns to Buchan and MacDiarmid. There were parallels in European regionalism, as well as in the mixed societies of the old Empire where 'received pronunciation' was a disadvantage. The British culture of the 'People's War' (1939-45) would prove as temporary as empire had been: without it prospects for federalism weren't good.

The present confrontation – English Conservatism lacking a Scottish mandate – shifts back to the 1630s and the Three Kingdoms situation, with Westminster using its reserved subjects as today's 'Lords of the Articles'. Its ambitions haven't checked the City or restored its own international clout, but Ireland couldn't rescue its economic miracle from its pluto-crats.

What lies ahead? The Anglo-Scottish union was

not grounded in a constitution, and in 1999-2010 the two countries, though held together by a British Labour government, saw development possibilities become quite different, as military and financial power ran out. Crucially, David Cameron in his coalition agreement with the LibDems, lost the key power of a British premier: control over when to dissolve Parliament.

On 15 October 2012 the British and Scottish governments agreed that a Referendum on Independence – Yes or No – would be held in Scotland, in autumn 2014. Initial polls showed only about a third favouring Yes, but there were political imponderables: both globally and in Britain. A century after 1914 English Europhobia seemed to mount, a feeling not shared in the north. Scotland would host the Commonwealth Games in Glasgow in 2014 (the 700th anniversary of Bannockburn). A 'new' electorate would enfranchise 16-year-olds. The issue was still open.

Even a No vote wouldn't end 'the march of a nation', but could the British Isles be federated? Or would a confederal 'league of states' within the islands be valuable as an alternative goal? This may in embryo lie with the British-Irish Secretariat, now based in Edinburgh. But the literal mechanism for any future is renewable power deployed against peak oil. Can this co-exist with Trident and giant aircraft carriers? Or must the last enchantments of empire yield to a European future?

* * *

Appendices

(1) HISTORY TO VISIT

Not a guide, but a follow-up to history in print or on film. The concentration is on 'Central Scotland' because most key events happened in places reachable in a day trip from Edinburgh, Glasgow or Dundee. For 'further afield' places, which need at least an overnight stop, scenery and recreation outweigh history.

Visit **www.clanscotland.org.uk** for more information.

CENTRAL SCOTLAND:

Ayr: Robert Burns's Country: his birthplace in Alloway, the ruined kirk and bridge out of 'Tam o' Shanter'. Robert Adam's nearby Culzean Castle shows the grand style of the lairds who patronised and exploited him.

Bute: Sail from Wemyss Bay (John Miller's splendid railway pier) to Rothesay, the Blackpool of Glasgow, and the extraordinary Florentine-gothic Mount Stuart mansion, built by the Marquess of Bute in 1880.

Clyde: The P.S. 'Waverley' (1947: last seagoing paddler in the world) visits the lochs and islands of the Clyde each summer. Arran, almost a miniature Scotland, Lochs Long and Fyne with fine mountains, Inveraray Castle, from which the Campbells ruled Scotland. The Trident submarines in Loch Long have enough nukes to blow us all to blazes.

Dundee: 'Juteopolis', the most imperial of Scots cities, made its cash from Calcutta hemp, pressed with whale oil. See the Verdant Factory and on the Tay the Antarctic research ship 'Discovery', based on whaling design. Famous for D.C. Thomson, keepers of Desperate Dan and Dennis the Menace. Across the Tay St Andrews, Scotland's first University (1411) and centre of Reformation and Mecca of Golf.

Edinburgh: With municipal (extinct) volcanoes, Arthur's Seat and Castlehill, medieval Old Town and classical New Town, grand museums and galleries, St Giles Kirk and Miralles' remarkable Parliament (2004). On outskirts Roslin, its ornate Chapel (1446) made legendary by Dan Brown, not to speak of Dolly the cloned sheep.

Falkirk and Linlithgow: Linlithgow Palace and Kirk show the Stewarts doing the grand style. Falkirk marked the start of smelting by coal with its Carron Ironworks, 1766. The Forth and Clyde Canal has the Falkirk Wheel (2000) connecting it to the Union Canal. At nearby Bo'ness see the Forth road and rail bridges and Scottish Railway Museum with working branch line. Blackness Castle was Elsinore in Mel Gibson's *Hamlet*; better than his *Braveheart*.

Fife: 'A beggar's mantle fringed with gold', reached by amazing bridges. Dunfermline famous as first royal capital, and birthplace of Andrew Carnegie; royal hunting palace at Falkland; Kirkcaldy for linoleum and Adam Smith; Anstruther for Scottish Fisheries Museum.

Glasgow: The magnificent St Mungo's Cathedral, (12th century) and Charles Rennie Mackintosh's 1910 Art College are European wonders. See also the Burrell Collection, Kelvingrove Art Galleries and Zahya Hadid's Riverside Museum of Transport.

Loch Lomond and the Trossachs: Made famous by Sir Walter Scott's 'The Lady of the Lake' and a halfday introduction to the Highlands by bus, boat and on Loch Katrine, vintage steamer called – you've guessed! – 'Sir Walter Scott'.

Melrose and Abbotsford: The Border Abbeys matured from being isolated hermitages to wool and wealth, Melrose being the most opulent. It marked the start of Scott's historical 'Waverley Novel' sequence (1814-27) whose income built his Abbotsford mansion (1812), almost a purpose-built literary factory.

New Lanark: Scotland's finest monument from the first industrial revolution, the four water-powered cotton mills built by David Dale in 1785, and used by Robert Owen for social experiment. Nearby Biggar is a small Victorian town with several museums.

Paisley: Famous for cotton-reels and fabulous shawls. **Port Glasgow:** (1683) marked the beginning of the Clyde's mercantile growth. **Greenock:** Boomed first with sugar, then with ships, then with IBM Europe. Where now?

Perth: Next to old coronation site of Scone. Gateway to Highlands with a huge station. North-east of Aviemore the whisky distilleries of the Spey valley. The Scots Reformation began in St. John's Kirk.

Stirling and Bannockburn: A key river-crossing to the north, commanded by an acropolis. At its bridge, Wallace's coup of 1297 destroyed the English army. In 1314, Bruce's victory confirmed Scots independence on Bannockburn field. Not far off the tiny 17th century trading port of Culross.

FURTHER AFIELD:

Aberdeen: City of Grey Granite, most astonishing at medieval St Machar's and Victorian Marischal College; oil has made it a bustling port (see the huge model production platform in Maritime Museum on the Quay); Queen Victoria's Balmoral, in castle country, is 60 miles west.

Inverness: Grand and pious Victorian city, blighted by supermarkets, but see Culloden Battlefield and Fort George and try to see Nessie (no-one has: making a non-thing as tourist attraction gets close to genius!) but gentle scenery and pleasant excursion boats on Telford's Caledonian Canal to Fort William. West and north lie the lands 'cleared' for sheep and deer.

Orkney and Shetland: Norse Scotland contains unequalled monuments from the Stone Age (Skara Brae, Maes Howe, Mousa Broch), the Viking age (Brough of Birsay) and the medieval grandeur of Kirkwall Cathedral and Earl's Palace. The culture of both archipelagos has thrived from being remote, and benefited from the oil boom.

West Highland Railway: Links Glasgow with the seaports of Oban and Mallaig, where ferries run to Mull and Columba's Iona and to Skye. From Kyle another spectacular line runs to Inverness and to the far north at Thurso and Wick. Bus to Ullapool for ferry to the Gaelic-speaking, tweed-weaving Outer Hebrides.

(2) THE SCOTTISH YEAR

These festivals, celebrations and events aren't just important in themselves; they show when places get booked out! For full details (and lots more events) visit **www.clanscotland.org.uk**.

January	Hogmanay (Yule, Dec 31 - Jan 1)
	Celtic Connections, Glasgow
	Burns Night (25 Jan)
	Up Helly AA! (Fire Festival), Shetland
February	Glasgow Film Festival
March	St Patrick's Day (17 Mar)
	Aberdeen Jazz Festival
	StAnza (Poetry Festival), St Andrews
	Ceilidh Culture, Edinburgh
	St Andrews Golf Festival
April	Beltane Fire Festival, Edinburgh
	Dumfries & Galloway Wildlife Festival
May	May Day / Labour Movement Marches
	Church of Scotland General Assembly
	Seven-a-side Borders Rugby
	Orkney Folk Festival
	Shetland Folk Festival
	Isle of Skye Accordion & Fiddle Festival
	Perth Festival of the Arts
	Dumfries and Galloway Arts Festival
	Islay Festival of Music and Malt

June	Border Common Ridings
	Peebles Beltane Festival
	St Magnus Festival, Orkney
	Royal Highland Show, Edinburgh
	Edinburgh International Film Festival
July	Holyrood Parliament in Recess
	Protestant 'marching season'
	T(ennents) in the Park (Kinross's 'Glastonbury')
	Borders Book Festival, Melrose
August	'Glorious Twelfth' Grouse-shooting season opens (12 Aug)
	'Cowal Fortnight' regatta, Clyde
	Holyrood Highland Games
	Festival of Politics, Edinburgh
	Edinburgh International, Fringe and Book Festivals
	Royal Edinburgh Military Tattoo
September	Wigtown Book Festival
	Holyrood Parliament in Session
October	Halloween, 'ghaists and bogles' not 'trick or treat' (31 Oct)
	Mod (Gaelic Language Festival) in Highland towns
November	Armistice Day (11 Nov)
	St Andrew's Day (30 Nov)
December	Christmas (25 Dec)

(3) TWENTY BOOKS ABOUT SCOTLAND

Sources:
Rosemary Goring, *Scotland: the Autobiography*, London: Penguin, 2008.
Louise Yeomans, *Reportage Scotland*, Edinburgh: Luath, 2000.

General and Political History
Michael Fry, *Patronage and Principle: A Political History of Modern Scotland*, Aberdeen University Press, 1987.
Michael Fry, *The Scottish Empire*, Edinburgh: Birlinn, 2001.
Richard Finlay, *Modern Scotland*, London: Profile, 2004.
RAB Houston and Bill Knox, eds., *The New Penguin History of Scotland*, London: Penguin, 2001.
Christopher Harvie, *A Floating Commonwealth*, Oxford, 2008.
James Mitchell, *Strategies for Self-Government*, Edinburgh: Polygon, 1996.
Kenneth O Morgan, ed., *The Oxford History of Britain*, Oxford UP, 1983.

Social History:
Bechhofer, McCrone and Paterson, *Living in Scotland*, Edinburgh University Press, 2004.
Tom Devine, *The Scottish Nation*, London: Penguin 1999.
Bill Knox, *Industrial Nation*, Edinburgh University Press, 1999.

John Ransom, *Iron Road: the Railway in Scotland* , Edinburgh: Birlinn, 2006.

Christopher Smout, *A History of the Scottish People, 1560-1830*, Glasgow: Collins, 1969.

Christopher Smout, *A Century of the Scottish People, l830-l950*, Glasgow: Collins, l986.

Cultural and Art History:

Cairns Craig et al., eds., *The History of Scottish Literature*, 4 Vols., Aberdeen University Press, 1988-1990.

Robert Crawford, *Scotland's Books*, Penguin, 2008.

Billy Kay, *The Scottish World*, Edinburgh: Mainstream, 2006.

Duncan Macmillan, *Scottish Art, 1460-1990*, Edinburgh: Mainstream, 1990.

Sean Connery and Murray Grigor, *Being a Scot*, London: Weidenfeld, 2008.

(4) TWELVE WEBSITES ABOUT SCOTLAND

www.clanscotland.org.uk

www.visitscotland.com

www.nts.org.uk

www.scottishparliament.uk

www.scotsman.com

www.historic-scotland.gov.uk

www.nms.ac.uk

www.travelinescotland.com

www.nationalgalleries.org

www.nls.uk

www.edinburghfestivals.co.uk

www.educationscotland.gov.uk/scotlandshistory/

Index